MYSTERY OF METAPHYSICS & EXISTENCE

Omar Lopez, PhD

MYSTERY OF METAPHYSICS & EXISTENCE

Cover Design by

www.srwalkerdesigns.com

ZADKIEL PUBLISHING

The genuine seeker has a "Constant and
passionate longing to break free from life's
sorrows... not by running away from it, but by
growing beyond his mind and by experiencing in
himself the reality of the Self which knows
neither birth nor death."
Sage Ramana Maharshi

Terms and Conditions

The nature of the sacred quest is such
that you may have a word, name, or
concept of what it is you are looking for,
some idea of what it is, how, and where it
may be found.
Tau Malachi (The Gospel of St Thomas)

ACKNOWLEDGMENTS

I would like to express my sincere gratitude to Dr. Norman W. Wilson, for providing his invaluable guidance, comments, and suggestions throughout the writing of this book. I especially want to thank the International Church of Metaphysical Humanism, Dr. Doug Kelley, Dr. Vicki Hunter, and Dr. Michael Kelley for providing such a wonderful academic program and for their support at Thomas Francis University. To my beautiful wife Denise, thank you for standing by my side and for giving me the motivation and encouragement in writing this book. To the Universal Life Church in Modesto, California, thank you for your support while I completed my Master's and Doctorate of Metaphysical Science degrees at your institution. Special thanks go to Stephen R. Walker from, S.R. Walker Designs, for his incredible work in designing the book cover. Last but not least, I want to thank www.pixabay.com and its artists for allowing me to use their photos and graphics.

Table of Contents

Foreword

Life is meaningful in what sense? What do we mean by consciousness? Why is there something, rather than nothing? Are there any nonphysical entities? There are probably a lot of other questions in your head right now. The problem is we are still missing pieces of the puzzle. It takes a thorough understanding of metaphysics to answer questions like these. Reading this book will allow you to gain a better understanding of what metaphysics is while logically trying to understand the world around you.

"In appearance, I'm a thing moving about in space. In reality, I am that moving space itself."
Douglas Harding

Chapter 1: Anthropic Principle

Metaphysics involves studying the nature of reality, either known or unknown, by exploring the nature of reality, metaphysics describes what is exactly real. In addition, it shows the relationship between matter and mind, consciousness and reality, and between potentiality and actuality. Metaphysics deals with some very abstract questions that many philosophers, physicists, and scientists believe have no logical or mathematical explanations.

**"METAPHYSICS, LIKE THE BRANCHES OF A TREE,
OPENS TO ALL THERE IS IN THE UNIVERSE AND BEYOND."**

Humans have contemplated the meaning of our life for decades. From philosophers debating whether their minds could be trusted to provide accurate interpretations of our reality to physicists attempting to interpret the weirder aspects of quantum physics and relativity, we've learned that some aspects of our universe appear to be objectively true for all observers, while others are subject to the influence and properties of the observer.

The Universe has a set of rules, and physicists have been able to decipher at least some of them. On a continuous, non-quantum level, we comprehend how gravity operates. We are familiar (mathematically), with a substantial number of the particles that exist (based on the Standard Model) and their interactions with the other fundamental forces. We know that we exist, made up of the same particles and subject to the same natural rules as everything else in the Universe.

The Universe is consistent with our existence at this precise position in space-time because we exist as observers, here and now, within it. And that our universe, including the fundamental parameters on which it depends, must exist in such a way that observers like ourselves at some point exist within it.

Today, these two statements are referred to, respectively, as the Weak Anthropic Principle and the Strong Anthropic Principle. They can enable us to make tremendously significant inferences and limits about the nature of our universe when applied appropriately.

Despite the fact that the scientific method and scientific tests and observations have revealed many of the fundamental physical rules and entities that govern our Universe, there is still much that we do not know.

Here is what our very existence may teach us about the nature of our reality. Consider these facts collectively: The Universe is governed by parameters, constants, and laws, within this universe, we exist, and the entirety of everything that determines how the universe functions must allow for the presence of beings like ourselves.

There appears to be a collection of straightforward, self-evident truths. We would not exist if it were physically impossible for beings like us to exist in the universe. If the features of the universe were incompatible with the presence of intelligent life, then it would have been impossible for our existence. But we have arrived. We exist. Consequently, our universe possesses the traits necessary for an intelligent observer to have conceivably evolved within it. The fact that humans exist and actively engage in viewing the cosmos suggests that the cosmos is designed in a way that makes our existence feasible.

Chapter 2: Branches of Metaphysics

Metaphysics is a branch of philosophy that has been around for centuries. Among all branches of philosophy, metaphysics is the most fundamental and essential. As opposed to other branches of philosophy, metaphysics deals with the vitality of the relationship between one's metaphysical perspective and how he/she interprets his universe and the world around him/her.

As far as metaphysicians are concerned, metaphysics looks for answers to the age-old questions like, "What's life's purpose?". Everything in the Universe is included in this question, from you and me to the subatomic particles in the quantum world and to reality itself. Different metaphysical views underlie every philosophical school and scientific discipline. Every school of thought in science and philosophy has its own uniqueness and distinction due to the diversity of metaphysical views.

Currently, metaphysics is regarded as modern science. Therefore, it could possibly be classed as an academic subject. Physics does not explain things beyond what can be understood by science, but metaphysics does.

Every person, regardless of whether they have studied the discipline or not, possesses a certain metaphysical system. It is called a metaphysical vision when people have a sense of reality and believe that things exist physically.

Additionally, the law that governs the universe and the world has a substantial significance in metaphysics. The causality law is regarded as the most important law among the others. According to it, every action results from an earlier action. There are two distinct perspectives on the world that result from this law of metaphysics. Depending on the predictability of the causation, it can result either in a primary or an endless cause. A belief that there is a primary cause requires a belief in the reality of God. In the belief in endless causation, those who believe in anarchic or chaotic explanations of the world's existence hold this belief.

In addition, metaphysics does not stop at these fields of study. Metaphysics is a very complex subject, so there is no definitive definition that can be offered from comprehensive studies. Since this area encompasses the whole of metaphysics, it simply does not make sense to separate it out. It makes no difference in any case what the case may be, one thing is certain - all humans possess a metaphysical perception that allows them to see the universe in a certain way that they may not or may not be aware of.

Branches of Metaphysics

Ontology, theology, and universal science are the three major categories of metaphysics. However, ontology is the most important branch of philosophy among the three. The goal of ontology is to determine what makes reality real. Theology is concerned with understanding who God is. Ontology is concerned with what makes reality what it is. Universal Science is the most difficult type of science to master. Among those topics are the origins of fundamental laws, the logic of the universe, and the origin of existence.

Ontology

Theology

Universal Science

It is possible to accelerate one's evolution through the application of metaphysical principles. You will be able to answer any questions you may have by having a basic understanding of this field. Moreover, you will be able to tell the difference between reality and fantasy.

Metaphysics encompasses a large range of topics. The more aspects you learn, the more comprehensive your understanding of the subject will be. There is something inspiring about metaphysics. This subject deals with both human spiritual and physical attributes. It starts where conventional psychology ends and finishes where the dogmas of religion begin.

You can benefit from learning about metaphysics in many ways. As you learn about the many laws that operate in the universe, you can learn about the existence of many cosmic laws. Also, you will be able to better understand the many phenomena that modern science cannot explain.

What is a Metaphysician?

A metaphysician is one who seeks to understand reality in its most basic form. Having these professionals on hand can help people understand the essence of metaphysics. One of their main tasks is to investigate every action in its entirety for truth.

Chapter 3: Meditation

Multiple methods of meditation are available. This can be performed through chanting, deep breathing, or prayer. If you follow one or more of these methods, you will gain a greater understanding of reality.

Through meditation, you can see other dimensions of reality, and your mind can become calmer. There are, on the other hand, types of meditation that serve no higher purpose than tranquilizing the mind. Some practitioners consider it to be therapeutic in nature. Different approaches are possible for achieving this goal.

It is intended that prayer be used as a conduit for communication with the Divine. A vital aspect of visualization is that it enables a person to have an outward manifestation of what they are imagining. It is important to add a term to mantra meditation that triggers your conscious mind to reflect. Metaphysically speaking, every type of meditation has its own advantages, and every method has a different benefit.

Metaphysics & Meditation

Metaphysical work demands the ability to calm the mind. In its first phase, it is thought to be the most vital. The idea of this meditation process is to balance your mind, body, and spirit. Keeping a quiet environment is essential, so choose a place that is free from distractions. As you take deep breaths, picture yourself somewhere that makes you happy. If you want, you can also play music produced for meditation. You can usually find free or affordable versions online.

In contrast, visualization in meditation is essential to healing in a metaphysical sense. It is essential that you have a mental representation of your accomplishment in your mind in order to achieve what you desire. Nevertheless, this representation would be nearly impossible to keep if you were confused or distracted. A religious image might be used as a visual icon in some cases, depending on the practice. Meditation can be accomplished using any or both of these techniques.

The concept of prayer is similar to that of metaphysical treatment, even if the practice differs. Ultimately, attaining your ultimate goal requires a metaphysical "energy" that comes from union with a Higher Power. In addition to treating, one's physical ailments, metaphysical awareness and meditation can also inspire one's spirit. To reach one's desires, it is essential to ensure that everyone involved gains something from the process.

Healing The Mind, Body & Soul Using Chakra

The most fundamental element of mental health, emotional stability, and physical wellbeing is chakra meditation. However, why? Due to the fact that the human chakras function as conductors, they are able to bring together earthly and heavenly energies. It is believed that vortexes of energy stimulate numerous endocrine glands throughout the body. In general, these devices come in the form of a funnel with a small tube inside.

Essentially, the chakras serve as portals through which the flow of life energy can be facilitated. As a result of such practices, a person's physical well-being and conscious awareness are enhanced. The activities are also beneficial to a person's mental, emotional, and physical capabilities.

In traditional thought, the aura represents the eighth chakra. The first chakra is usually concerned with the outer world. Between the knees and the thighs, this region of the body occupies the middle of the body. The 7th chakra is located on top of your head. The remaining 7 chakras are located on your spine, your neck, and your skull. A subtle-energy worker can still recognize chakras even if they cannot be seen with the naked eye.

Multiple benefits can be derived from metaphysical meditation. No matter what type of meditation you practice, you'll always come away feeling refreshed and renewed with a better ability to concentrate. There are a number of benefits to meditating, which you should know about:

Mediation Promotes General Wellness and Improves Health-Meditation induces a state of concentration that enhances blood flow and nutrient absorption. The benefits also extend to physical health and strength.

Enhances concentration - This benefit applies to both mental and physical issues. The nervous system of people who meditate regularly is also in good shape.

Reduces your oxygen consumption - Meditating reduces your oxygen consumption and deepens your breathing. Additionally, as your heart rate and blood pressure are reduced as you improve the efficiency and strength of blood flow.

Avoid Heart Attacks - If you meditate regularly, you will reduce the chances of contracting heart failure. Serotonin, a brain chemical, is also produced in your body when you meditate. This helps boost your mood and behavior.

Developing a state of relaxation through this healing process helps reduce anxiety and muscle tension. Chronic headaches and muscle aches can be alleviated as well.

It is evident that these various benefits provide you with both mental and physical relaxation. No matter which type of metaphysical meditation you practice, you are likely to have Positive results are achieved.

Chapter 4: Precognition

The ability to view into the future is an inborn one that almost every human possesses, despite it being associated with psychics. Sadly, most people haven't recognized whether they should use it or not.

There is a lot of complexity involved with precognition. Most of the time, metaphysical protocols and applications are involved. Today, the majority of experts in this field learn precognition techniques via private institutions and churches, workshops, retreat centers, the online web and books like this one. Others, however, choose to acquire this ability through specific sources of information. Everyone has the ability to see into the future. To do so, you should remain open-minded and persist in your efforts. Unique in that it provides the viewer or other involved individual with the ability to intuitively experience events, emotions, places, people, energy, ideas, emotions, abstractions, dimensions, vortices, and activities selected by them. Learn how to conduct a remote viewing by reading this description. Practicing precognition techniques does not require a great deal of expertise. In order for it to be successful, however, it must be conducted in accordance with a specific process and intention.

Below are some instructions for you. Follow these steps:

Step 1: Find a Quiet Environment – The quiet environment necessary for this technique is the same as for other psychic abilities. When your environment is peaceful, you can tap into your intuitive side more easily. Make sure you are completely alone before taking a walk outside in a quiet area. You must concentrate intensely before beginning. You need to choose a position that makes you feel comfortable and relaxed for best results. If you are sitting on the floor, you can turn your back to the floor and relax.

Step 2: Relax Your Body – If you are having trouble with concentrating, take a deep breath and position your tongue just behind your middle teeth on the roof of your mouth. Slowly and rhythmically maintain this posture. Whenever you breathe, feel your body getting fresh air. Visualize yourself getting a breath of fresh air when you breathe. Also visualize how the fresh air is cleansing your body while the anxiety is leaving you relaxed with a deep sense of well-being. Maintain this visualization for at least 10 minutes.

Step 3: Relax Your Mind – In order to completely relax your body, you have to put all your worries and doubts aside. You should also keep your mind focused on what you are doing. Be patient with yourself once thoughts still pop into your head. Focus on clearing your conscious mind and be patient.

Step 4: Pick a Structure That Makes You Happy – Take a moment to consider something that makes you happy. It can be a place, an individual, or something unique created by you. Whenever you are thinking about it, you should never allow your consciousness to fill in with any other thoughts. Instead, you should let the subconscious mind do the work. During the process of concentrating, certain thoughts and feelings will arise in your subconscious. In addition to knowing the taste and smell of the product, it is important to consider its size and color.

Step 5: Write Everything Down – After you have opened your eyes, jot down all the details you have gathered about what you visioned in your mind. Make sure to include each and every emotion you feel, observe, and think. You should use this information to find out as much as you can concerning the vision you receive. This ability can be mastered easily by following these procedures again and again. Practice makes perfect, and you will be more accurate the more you do it.

Chapter 5: Your Space and Time

It's good to establish your own space and time to restore your peace of mind. Additionally, you will also feel more empowered and regain your sense of self. The purpose of exploring the sanctuary is to develop a bond between the Soul and the Divine. Having a spiritual sense goes beyond emotional and psychological needs. As well as this, it is a biological necessity, as all your mental, energetic, and physical abilities are combined.

It's not easy to make a room where you can reflect. Nevertheless, if you know what steps to take and how to go about it, it can be simple. Consider these five ways to create sacred space:

Make a self-nutrition space in your living area or turn a guest room or attic into a self-feeding space. When you hold a sacred space in your heart, it sets the tone for your ultimate purpose.

The environment will be marked as a place of privacy through the use of a curtain, screen, beads. A space for inner guidance and knowledge may be created in this environment. Aside from drawing, writing, painting, you can also listen to birds singing outside your window.

Create a serene setting by placing pillows on the floor so that you can pray, meditate, and contemplate in peace. A comfortable chair is also important for supporting the back.

To bring the energy of spirituality to an altar, arrange spiritual objects on it. It's only necessary to use a specific fabric for an altar and a small table.

It will also be inspirational to listen to soft music or read an insightful book. These activities will help to increase your energy and feel relaxed.

It is possible to place numerous objects in a sacred place. There are scented candles available to suit your tastes. If you burn them during meditation, they help you focus. Be sure to place the candle securely and away from combustible materials.

If you want to get the most out of your sacred space, I would recommend placing different crystals within the room. There are 7 Chakra stones a metaphysician or reiki healer must own. The 7 Chakra Stones are as follow: Green Fluorite (Heart Chakra), Amethyst (Third Eye Chakra), Red Jasper (Root Chakra), Tiger's Eye Stone (Solar Plexus Chakra), Sodalite (Throat Chakra), Rock Quartz (Crown Chakra), Red Aventurine (Sacral Chakra).

Adding scent to your environment is also possible with scented essential oils. Besides burning natural oils, plants are also good choices for a sacred space. Your sanctuary can be enhanced by adding a sweet smell and vibrant colors using these plants. Plants also purify the air.

You can also add desktop water to make your place of sacredness more inviting. A water fountain provides calming sounds and removes other noises from the environment. Your sacred space will also be energized by the sound of water.

When you want to achieve peace of mind and relieve your stress, it is vital that you create your own sacred space. For example, try to imagine a room with more than one screaming child. What would you think if you had a room like this to refresh your mind? You must ensure that no one disturbs you if you want the environment to be tranquil. Within your room, you can have a restful sleep, and you can do anything you want without being distracted by anything in the surrounding world.

Many people prefer to hire an interior decorator as part of their effort to create the best-sacred space possible. The way to transform your room into a sanctified space does not require you to spend a great deal of money. You can accomplish it all by yourself within a short period of time if you use your creativity.

Chapter 6: Finding Your Inner Self

It is often the guidance of your inner self that leads you to take steps that are in alignment with who you are and who you are becoming. When these steps are taken, you will feel at peace. Despite the fact that you want to try new things, even though your inner guidance tells you to do so, you feel that you are lacking in self-confidence. In this case, you'll doubtless ask yourself, "how do I develop self-confidence?"

When you start inner guidance, it's crucial that you're in a good mood. The way you feel will largely determine how well you perform. You should also seek out a place where you can work in peace and quiet without interruption. Don't forget to prepare a notebook or pencil for writing down essential ideas. You can also use your smartphone or a personal voice recorder to record your voice instead.

It is important to imagine how good you feel when you receive answers or turn inward. In addition, you should be aware that the longer you drift from your core, the longer it takes you to learn. You must also recognize that as you transform within, you may need to let go of the negative emotions from the day

What Should You Do When Turning to Your Inner Guide?

Slowly is the key. Stay calm and be aware of being in a quiet and safe environment. As well as becoming aware of your body, you need to learn to relax and become comfortable. The representations your mind provides you with the need to also be taken into consideration. It is not uncommon for your mind to provide images that describe your desires. Make sure to write these down for later reference.

Review What You Wrote

Check out what you wrote. In order to determine whether the ideas are rational and healthy, it is necessary to apply rationality principles.

Be sure to learn the skill of bringing your inner voice to life. Don't forget to put those good ideas into action. There are also many workshops available that can help you learn rational thinking, solve your emotional problems, relax, succeed, set goals, and so on. Participating in these workshops will push you toward your desired goal.

Tips for Your Inner Guidance

You can tap into your inner guidance by following these simple tips. You can follow these tips to tap into your inner guidance:

Learn inner guidance - Inner guidance is similar to the radiant light that shines through a garden. Your garden can enhance your ability to perceive light and help you to find your center when it is clean and organized.

Chant the sound OM. Chanting the sound OM before practicing remote viewing helps raise your natural vibrational frequency.

Stay Calm - You need to clear your mind of all worries and attempt to remain calm. The inner guidance you hear will soon become more apparent.

Be patient - You will hear different voices from different directions during your first inner guidance. It is important not to give up, however. The only thing you have to do is be patient and wait for the process to take place.

"MIND MAY BE TRANSMITTED FROM STATE TO STATE; DEGREE TO DEGREE; CONDITION TO CONDITION; POLE TO POLE; VIBRATION TO VIBRATION."   - THE KYBALION

Chapter 7: Extrasensory Perception

Extrasensory perception or ESP, also called sixth sense, is a claimed paranormal ability pertaining to reception of information not gained through the recognized physical senses, but sensed with the mind. extrasensory perception (ESP) is a type of perception that doesn't involve the normal senses. Usually, telepathy, which is the transference of thoughts from one person to another, clairvoyance, which is the supernatural awareness of objects or events that other people might not know about, and precognition, which is knowing the future, fall into this category. Since the late 1800s, scientists have been looking into these and other similar things. Most of the evidence comes from card-guessing experiments. Subjects try to guess correctly, under controlled conditions, what the symbols on cards are that they can't see. A higher-than-chance percentage of right guesses over a statistically significant number of trials is thought to be proof of ESP. Even though many scientists still don't believe in ESP, people who say they have it are sometimes used by teams looking for people or things that have gone missing or have no logical explanation.

ESP or extrasensory perception can be boosted through remote influencing, a mental technique. This is accomplished through reprogramming the subconscious mind. The ability to influence someone else's decision from a distance is also part of this, as it involves suggesting actions that the individual should take. Psychics and magic communities have always been concerned about remote influence. Remote influence has been practiced for several years now. Voodoo and shamanism incorporate different forms of remote influence into their ancient traditions. Historically, they have been used to curse, heal and wage war.

Being a master of your future begins with you. Any person who is able to see and hear will be able to do this. Using this technique requires no one to be a magician.

Forget all the worldly knowledge that thou hast
acquired…then will thou get the divine wisdom.
Ramakrishna

Manifesting Your Affirmations

The process of manifesting your desire is quite straightforward. Simply state your goal in an affirmation and watch it happen. You should prepare your indication before you begin. Consider the possibilities of having a better car sitting in your driveway, for instance. In the fabric of space and time you already have all of the things you desire. The Universe simply needs to know what you desire.

It is initially important to get into a comfortable state of alpha to theta. Focus on breathing two or three times from your abdominal region as a quick and easy way to accomplish this. Put your hand in front of your face and visualize a white cloud of light energy. You are now living in the matrix of intelligence.

As well as visualizing the condition in your life, you must imagine a symbol of it. If you wanted to represent money with the dollar symbol and health with the scale symbol, for example. If you wanted to say "I attract money", for example. Once you have observed the cloud, you must change its color. You choose the color depending on what you prefer. Green, for example, represents wealth, while orange symbolizes health and pink represents love. Make sure that you do this every day for at least eight minutes to avoid becoming exhausted.

"Men at some time are masters of their fates:
The fault, dear Brutus, is not in our stars,
But in ourselves, that we are underlings."
-Julius Caesar, Act I, Scene II
— William Shakespeare

Chapter 8: Existence

Defining Reality

What does real mean? What about trees, animals, and humans? Do they exist? Does God exist? You'll know the answers to these questions once you grasp the concept of reality. It is always beneficial to understand a reality so that your beliefs can be strengthened and the beliefs of others can be resolved.

Concrete things represent a fact or thing, and its Latin meaning is "res". In addition, it pertains to reality itself. In contrast, absolute reality refers to those things that exist at their most fundamental level. You may be conscious or unconscious, or have a highly systematic approach if you do not possess a complete understanding of reality. The organized approach guides you in your actions.

The perception of reality works as a filter and monitors the sensory data you receive. The foundation also tells us what we should do with our lives, what we believe in, how we feel, and much more.

Understanding Reality

Humans need to be able to comprehend reality accurately. One of the problems in comprehending reality is, who's reality is the right one? Yours or mine? Despite the diverse and contradictory claims of the secular world, modern science and religion can be reconciled. A systematic framework that complements your faith, thoughts, and life also offers you the opportunity to be everlastingly strong.

Understanding reality allows you to make more educated choices since you understand what is real and what is not. Additionally, you can remove false beliefs and misconceptions that can lead to disappointment, discomfort, and anxiety. Understanding reality in depth can also give you a sense of well-being. Furthermore, you will gain a deeper understanding of people, which will make you a more mature person.

Are we living inside a computer game? Is the whole universe, from the smallest atom to the biggest galaxy, just a computer program being simulated on the hard drive of an all-powerful being? At first glance, the idea of simulated reality seems silly, but think about how far computer games, virtual reality, and robotics have come. Are we, by accident, making the case for simulation theory stronger?

David Chalmers of NYU — suggest that increasingly bizarre events in the "real" world may be evidence that our universe is someone else's simulation. Beyond universe simulation, these events may represent divergent "points" in reality; in another universe the mix-up didn't happen. In another reality, Donkey Kong actually won.

The Case for Simulation Theory

This argument, which is also called the simulation hypothesis, is simple: All of reality is, in fact, a computer simulation, probably run by a very powerful supercomputer. In just a few short decades, people have been able to make machines that can learn and copy many basic human intelligence traits. If computers keep getting better at the rate they are now, it could be easy for future humans or other intelligent life to make a simulation of the universe.

The Simulation Theory has been backed by a number of well-known scientists and innovators. During the 2016 Isaac Asimov Memorial Debate, Neil deGrasse Tyson said that there was a 50/50 chance that our universe is a simulation. This was reported by Scientific American. Even though our DNA is 98 percent the same, he said that the big difference in intelligence between chimpanzees and humans showed that a creature with many times our intelligence could exist and possibly run simulations.

From the point of view of why people exist and why we want to learn more about the universe, this debate about simulations is mostly academic. We still seem to have free will and the ability to look into our own reality to see if any basic scientific truths come out. If we're just a simulation, the results of our work might change, but that doesn't make them less important.

Another option for existence is the Multiverse Theory, where our universe is just one of many with its own set of physical laws and properties. And what's more simulation-like than running multiple instances of something to see which one works best? In this theory, every choice, no matter how minuscule, could create its own universe. In his book Something Deeply Hidden, Sean Carroll asserts that quantum mechanics describes not just very small things but everything, including us. "As far as we currently know," he writes, "quantum mechanics isn't just an approximation to the truth; it is the truth." And however preposterous it might seem, a multiverse, Carroll argues, is an inescapable consequence of quantum mechanics.

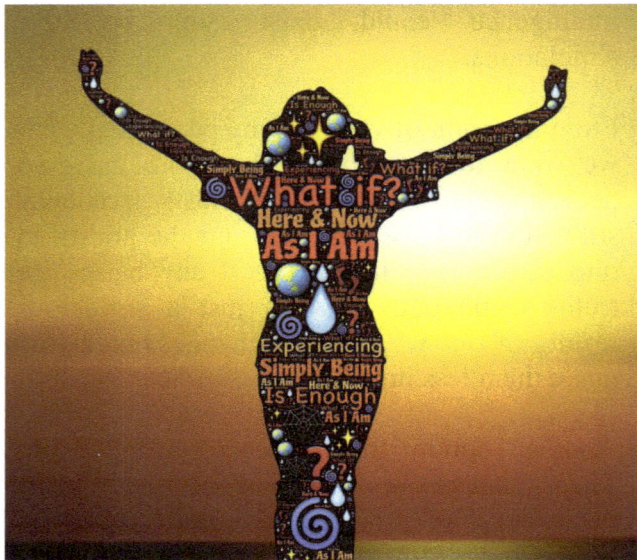

"The here and now is all we have, and if we play it right it's all we'll need."
— Ann Richards

"It's hard to build models of inflation that don't lead to a multiverse. It's not impossible, so I think there's still certainly research that needs to be done. But most models of inflation do lead to a multiverse, and evidence for inflation will be pushing us in the direction of taking [the idea of a] multiverse seriously."
— Alan H. Guth

Chapter 9: Consciousness

It is elusive to understand what consciousness is. This is a state of being in which one has crystal clear ideas about what is going on in the world. One can understand what is going to happen in the future because one is in the present. It is also possible to sense the good and the bad in what you feel and think.

Consciousness is an extremely complex subject. The nervous system has multiple interconnected networks that influence consciousness. In a healthy individual, this shade of consciousness changes throughout the day and night. There is no such thing as being conscious of your fears. This simply means you are able to perceive them. Consciousness does not possess mass or portion, even if it keeps expanding through experiential methods. This fact makes it impossible to define it scientifically. Physical reality is possible because consciousness uses matter as a covering. It is critical that you gain more knowledge on how to manage self-consciousness if you don't know how to control it. For humans to understand others and communicate, self-consciousness is necessary. Developing a strong belief about yourself and understanding yourself are the first step.

In appearance I am a thing moving about in space.
In reality,
I'm that unmoving space itself.
Douglas Harding

Never criticize yourself, constantly seek approval, or be doubtful of yourself. Never stop loving yourself for who you are.

The Subconscious Mind

Consciousness and subconsciousness are terms used to indicate the different aspects of the mind. In turn, the subconscious uses symbols and images to convey meaning.

Psychological expressions in the subconscious are primarily conceptual thought, beliefs, and creative ideas. These expressions can also be linked to life experiences and follow generic behavioral patterns.

Conversely, consciousness is what enables your awareness or waking state to come into being. People's sensory experiences provide them with the details of their environment.

Conclusion

It is essential for men to not take any man-made fact for granted when they are creative. They need an "unborrowed vision". This concept pertains to the ability to challenge what others see as unchanging, eternal facts. There is no need to judge only what has been created by man. In addition to their creativity, they have the capacity to reorganize reality in new ways. It is through their imagination that they accomplish this.

There is no conflict between creation and the fact that the given is complete from a metaphysical point of view. The power of rearranging reality is not to change reality, but to reorganize what already exists. To achieve their goals, this is the key purpose.

Men create their own rules to manage themselves, and metaphysics defines them as different rules. There are different types of confusion concerning the two. In that men's preferences aren't necessary, the concept of man-made metaphysics is a fundamental difference. Let's say for example that a certain law is selected. Several people claim that the way things are can't be changed because they're the way they are.

It is believed that the Universe is created by human thought. Metaphysics has been criticized for making the assumption that a man can act and create reality in such a way, a flaw that is often made. To continue living, that man needs to act in accordance with his awareness.

You will be able to see how metaphysics, reality, consciousness, and other related details relate to each other after reading this book. I would want to take a step back and discuss the primary motivation behind my decision to write this book in the first place. The many changes in my personality, opinions, and interests that have taken place over the course of the years that I've spent as a student in metaphysics provided the impetus for the desire. The two that stand out as the most significant are the fact that I became a Scientific Pantheist during my studies in the field and the strong urge to learn about reality (what is accurate about the cosmos and where we fit into it?). An attitude that says: "Well, maybe what I believe is wrong, but I'm comfortable believing it," might be contrasted with the aspiration to find out what is actually happening in the world. It is simple to understand how having a distorted perception of the world might put a person in jeopardy. I will be the first to agree that when it comes to some of our other ideas, this threat is not as readily apparent; but the idea that we have of who we are serves as the foundation for almost everything else that we do.

I don't think there is only one universe or that there is no God. Science or religion can't prove either that

God exists or that there are many universes, so the only sensible position I see is an agnostic point of view. I think multiverse theories have some value. Especially when told by a talented writer like Sean Carroll, they spark our imaginations and make us think about how big the world is. In a good way, they make us feel really, really small.

Parmenides

"out of nothing nothing comes"

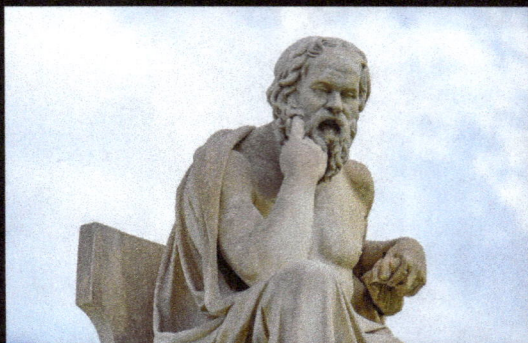

Socrates

"The only true wisdom is in knowing
you know nothing."

Plato

"How can you prove whether at this moment we are sleeping, and all our thoughts are a dream; or whether we are awake, and talking to one another in the waking state?"

Aristotle

"Happiness is the meaning and the purpose of life, the whole aim and end of human existence."

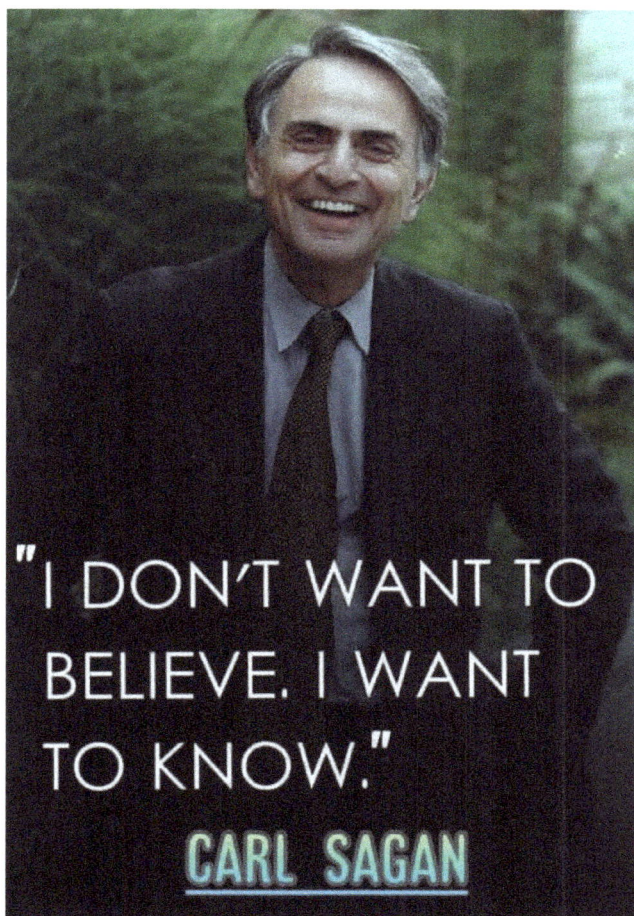

"I DON'T WANT TO BELIEVE. I WANT TO KNOW."

CARL SAGAN

About the Author

Omar Lopez from a young age has always been fascinated by science, physics, and the world of the unknown.

For the past 25 years, Omar has worked as an electronic technician. The questions Omar asked himself were getting deeper and deeper, pondering for days on end about "How does the Universe work? What is life's purpose?

At the age of 40, his passion for ontology led him to dedicate his studies to the fields of science, astrophysics, and metaphysics, and earned his Bachelor's of Metaphysical Humanistic Science degree at Thomas Francis University, and his Master's & Doctorate of Metaphysical Science degrees at Universal Life Church in Modesto California, where he is an ordained minister in good standing.

His experiences and studies within his field, have led him to share information about what he has learned throughout the years with as many people as possible and in the simplest way possible.

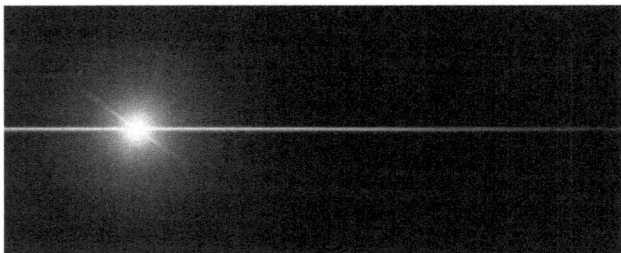

Metaphysical Dictionary

Altered States of Consciousness
Any state which is significantly different from a normative waking beta wave state. The expression was coined by Charles Tart and describes induced changes in one's mental state, almost always temporary. A synonymous phrase is "altered states of awareness".

Angels
An angel is a supernatural being found in many religions. In scripture, they typically act as messengers, as held by the three prominent monotheistic faiths, Christianity, Judaism and Islam.

Apparition
An apparition is an appearance to a human of a ghost.

Astral
Relating to a subtle body and plane of existence that coexist with and survive the death of the human physical body.

Astral body
The astral body refers to the concept of a subtle body which exists alongside the physical body, as a vehicle of the soul or consciousness. It is usually

understood as being of an emotional nature and, as such, it is equated to the desire body or emotional body.

Astral plane
The astral plane, also called the astral world or desire world, is a plane of existence according to esoteric philosophies, some religious teachings and New Age thought.

Astral Projection
Out-of-body experiences (OBEs) achieved either awake or via lucid dreaming, deep meditation, or use of psychotropics. The consciousness or soul has transferred into an astral body which moves in the astral plane.

Aura
Energy field emanating from the surface of a person or object. This emanation is visualized as an outline of cascading color and may be held to represent soul vibrations, chakric emergence, or a reflection of surrounding energy fields.

Automatic Writing
Automatic writing is the process of writing material that does not come from the conscious thoughts of the writer. The writer's hand forms the message, and the person is unaware of what will be written. It is sometimes done in a trance state. Other times the writer is aware (not in a trance) of their

surroundings but not of the actions of their writing hand.

Chakra
Nexus of biophysical energy residing in the human body, aligned in an ascending column from the base of the spine to the top of the head. In various traditions chakras are associated with multiple physiological functions, an aspect of consciousness, a classical element, and other distinguishing characteristics.

Channeling
Process of receiving messages or inspiration from invisible beings or spirits.

Christ
The word is often misunderstood to be the surname of Jesus due to the numerous mentions of Jesus Christ in the Christian Bible. The word is in fact a title, hence its common reciprocal use Christ Jesus, meaning The Anointed One, Jesus. Followers of Jesus became known as Christians because they believed that Jesus was the Christ, or Messiah, prophesied about in the Tanakh (which Christians term the Old Testament).

Clairvoyance
Extra-sensory perception whereas a person perceives distant objects, persons, or events, including perceiving an image hidden behind opaque objects and the detection of types of energy

not normally perceptible to humans. Typically, such perception is reported in visual terms, but may also include auditory impressions (sometimes called clairaudience) or kinesthetic impressions.

Demon
In religion, folklore, and mythology a demon (or daemon) is a supernatural being that has generally been described as a malevolent spirit, and in Christian terms it generally understood as an angel not following God.

Demonology
Demonology is the systematic study of demons or beliefs about demons. Insofar as it involves exegesis, demonology is an orthodox branch of theology.

Devil
The Devil is a title given to the supernatural entity, who, in Christianity, Islam, and other religions, is a powerful, evil entity and the tempter of humankind. The Devil commands a force of lesser evil spirits, commonly known as demons.

Ectoplasm
Form of dense bio-energy liberated by the materialization of ghosts. Also, a substance supposed to emanate from the body of the medium during a trance.

EMF (Electro-magnetic Field)
Classically, the electromagnetic field is a physical influence (a field) that permeates through all of space, and which arises from electrically charged objects and describes one of the four fundamental forces of nature - electromagnetism. Ghost activities can sometimes causes changes in the electro-magnetic field and measured with an EMF meter.

Empath
Possesses the ability to sense the emotions of other sentient life forms.

Entity
An entity is something that has a distinct, separate existence.

Esoteric (Esotericism)
The term Esotericism refers to the doctrines or practices of esoteric knowledge, or otherwise the quality or state of being described as esoteric, or obscure. Esoteric knowledge is that which is specialised or advanced in nature, available only to a narrow circle of "enlightened", "initiated", or highly educated people. In contrast, exoteric knowledge is knowledge that is well-known or public.

ESP (Extra Sensory Perception)
Perception that involves awareness of information about something (such as a person or event) not

gained through the senses and not deducible from previous experience. Classic forms of ESP include telepathy, clairvoyance, and precognition.

Etheric plane
In Theosophy, the etheric plane is related to the Prana principle and is understood as the vital, life-sustaining force of living beings and the vital energy in all natural processes of the universe.

Etheric body
The etheric body, or vital body is one of the subtle bodies in esoteric philosophies, in some religious teachings and in New Age thought. It is understood as a sort of life force body or aura that constitutes the "blueprint" of the physical body, and which sustains the physical body.

Evil
In religion and ethics, evil refers to the morally or ethically objectionable behavior or thought; behavior or thought which is hateful, cruel, excessively sexual, or violent, devoid of conscience.

EVP (Electronic Voice Phenomena)
Electronic voice phenomena (EVP) is the communication by spirits through radios, tape recorders, or other electronic audio devices. Also, when anomalous voices of supernatural origin, are heard on audio recordings.

Exorcism
The practice of evicting demons or other evil spiritual entities which have possessed a person or object. The practice is quite ancient and still part of the belief system of many religions. The person performing the exorcism, known as an exorcist, is often a priest, or an individual thought to be graced with special powers or skills. The exorcist may use religious material, such as prayers and set formulas, gestures, symbols, icons, amulets, etc. The exorcist often invokes some supernatural power to actually perform the task.

Ghost
A ghost is a non-corporeal manifestation of the spirit or soul of a dead person which has remained on Earth after death.

Ghost Hunting
Ghost hunting is the process of investigating an alleged haunting. Typically, a 'hunting party' will involve 4-8 individuals who work as a team to collect evidence of paranormal activity. Each team member performs duties that are related to their particular field of expertise or interest. It is common practice for ghost hunters to behave in a scientific manner as they observe and record data using a variety of electronic gadgets, such as; EMF Meters, digital thermometers, infrared and night vision cameras, handheld video cameras, digital audio recorders, and computers.

God

The name God refers to the deity held by monotheists to be the supreme reality. God is generally regarded as the sole creator of the universe. Theologians have ascribed certain attributes to God, including omniscience, omnipotence, omnipresence, perfect goodness, divine simplicity, and eternal and necessary existence.

Guardian Spirit (Guardian Angel)

A guardian angel is a spirit who protects and guides a particular person.

Haunting

To inhabit, visit, or appear to in the form of a ghost or other supernatural being.

Heaven

Heaven is a plane of existence in religions and spiritual philosophies, typically described as the holiest possible place, accessible by people according to various standards of divinity (goodness, piety, etc.) Christians generally hold that it is the afterlife destination of those who have accepted Jesus Christ as their savior.

Hell

Hell, according to many religious beliefs, is an afterlife of suffering where the wicked or unrighteous dead are punished. Hells are almost always depicted as underground. Christianity and Islam traditionally depict hell as fiery, Hells from other traditions, however, are sometimes cold and gloomy.

Hypnagogia (Hypnogogic)
Hypnagogia are the experiences a person can go through in the hypnagogic (or hypnogogic) state, the period of falling asleep. Hypnagogic sensations collectively describe the vivid dream-like auditory, visual, or tactile sensations that can be experienced in a hypnagogic or hypnopompic state.

Hypnosis
Psychological condition of altered state of consciousness in which some people may be induced to show various differences in behavior and thinking, like heightened suggestibility and receptivity to direction.

Hypnotherapy
Hypnotherapy is therapy that is undertaken with a subject in hypnosis. A person who is hypnotized displays certain unusual characteristics and propensities, compared with a non-hypnotized subject, most notably hyper-suggestibility, which some authorities have considered a sine qua non of hypnosis.

Incarnation
Incarnation, which literally means enfleshment, refers to the conception, and live birth of a sentient

creature (generally human being) who is the material manifestation of an entity or force whose original nature is immaterial.

Incorporeal
Incorporeal, from Latin, means without the nature of a body or substance. The idea of the incorporeal refers to the notion that there is an incorporeal realm or place, that is distinct from the corporeal or material world.

Intuition
Intuition is an immediate form of knowledge in which the knower is directly acquainted with the object of knowledge. Intuition differs from all forms of mediated knowledge, which generally involve conceptualizing the object of knowledge by means of rational/analytical thought processes.

Intuitive
A person sensitive to the feelings of other life forms, as well as signals of nature.

Jinn
Genie is the English term for the Arabic (jinn). In pre-Islamic Arabian mythology and in Islam, a jinni (also "djinni" or "djini") is a member of the jinn (or "djinn"), a race of supernatural creatures.

Karma
Karma is the concept of "action" or "deed" in Dharmic religions understood as denoting the entire

cycle of cause and effect described in Hindu, Jain, Sikh and Buddhist philosophies. Karma is believed to be a sum of all that an individual has done, is currently doing and will do. The effects of all deeds actively create past, present and future experiences, thus making one responsible for one's own life, and the pain and joy it brings to others.

Kirlian photography

Kirlian photography refers to a form of contact print photography, theoretically associated with high-voltage. It is named after Semyon Kirlian, who in 1939 accidentally discovered that if an object on a photographic plate is connected to a source of high voltage, small corona discharges (created by the strong electric field at the edges of the object) create an image on the plate.

Magic

Magic and sorcery are the influencing of events, objects, people and physical phenomena by mystical, paranormal or supernatural means. The terms can also refer to the practices employed by a person to wield this influence, and to beliefs that explain various events and phenomena in such terms.

Manifestation

The materialized form of a spirit.

Medium
A person who possess the ability to communicate with spirits of deceased people (and sometimes pets). Some mediums claim to be able to channel the spirit, by allowing the deceased to speak or write messages using the medium's body.

Metaphysics
Metaphysics is the branch of philosophy concerned with explaining the ultimate nature of reality, being, and the world. More recently, the term "metaphysics" has also been used more loosely to refer to "subjects that are beyond the physical world".

Near-death experience
A near-death experience (NDE) is an experience reported by a person who nearly died, or who experienced clinical death and then revived. The experience has become more common in recent times, especially since the development of cardiac resuscitation techniques. Popular interest in near-death experiences was sparked by Raymond Moody Jr's 1975 book Life after Life and the founding of the International Association for Near-death Studies (IANDS) in 1978.

Occult
The word has many uses in the English language, popularly meaning 'knowledge of the paranormal'. For most practicing occultists it is simply the study

of a deeper spiritual "reality" that extends beyond pure reason and the physical sciences.

Orb
Name given to typically circular anomalies appearing in photographs. In photography and video, orbs appear to be balls, diamonds, or smears of light with an apparent size in the image ranging from a golf ball to a basketball. Orbs sometimes appear to be in motion, leaving a trail behind them.

Ouija
Ouija refers to the belief that one can receive messages during a séance by the use of a Ouija board (also called a talking board or spirit board) and planchette. The fingers of the participants are placed on the planchette which then moves about a board covered with numbers, letters and symbols so as to spell out messages. Ouija Board is a trademark for a talking board currently sold by Parker Brothers. The term "Ouija" is derived from the French "oui" (for "yes") and the German/Dutch "ja" (also for "yes").

Out-of-body experience
An out-of-body experience (OBE or sometimes OOBE) is an experience that typically involves a sensation of floating outside of one's body and, in some cases, seeing one's physical body from a place outside one's body.

Paranormal

Paranormal is an umbrella term used to describe a wide variety of reported anomalous phenomena. According to the Journal of Parapsychology, the term paranormal describes "any phenomenon that in one or more respects exceeds the limits of what is deemed physically possible according to current scientific assumptions."

Parapsychology

Parapsychology is the study of seeming mental awareness of or influence upon external objects, without any physical or energetic means of causation which scientists currently understand. Most objects of study fall within the realm of "mind-to-mind" influence (such as extra-sensory perception and telepathy), "mind-to-environment" influence (such as psychokinesis) and "environment-to-mind" (such as hauntings). Collectively, these abilities are often referred to as "psionics". Another definition of parapsychology is the scientific study of paranormal phenomena.

Past life regression (therapy)

Past life regression is a technique used by some hypnotherapists to try to get clients to remember their past lives. Implicit in this procedure is the spiritual belief that souls exist and come back many times, living in different times and places, experiencing different genders, races, social classes and so forth in an attempt to learn.

Prayer
Prayer is an active effort to communicate with a deity or spirit either to offer praise, to make a request, seek guidance, confess sins, or simply to express one's thoughts and emotions.

Poltergeist
Spirit or ghost that manifests by moving and influencing inanimate objects (rather than through visible presence or vocalization). Stories featuring poltergeists typically focus heavily on raps, thumps, knocks, footsteps, and bed-shaking, all without a discernable point of origin or physical reason for occurrence. Many accounts of poltergeist activity detail objects being thrown about the room, furniture being moved, and even people being levitated.

Possession
Concept of supernatural and/or superstitious belief systems whereby gods, demons or other disincarnate entities may temporarily take control of a human body, resulting in noticeable changes in behavior. The concept of spiritual possession exists in many contemporary religions and can also be seen in the mythology and folklore of many cultures. Various forms and denominations of Christianity have developed practices for driving out spirit, most notably Roman Catholicism; there exists a Roman Catholic International Association of Exorcists.

Portal

A doorway, entrance, or gate between two worlds, the physical and the spiritual.

Psychic

person who possesses extra-sensory abilities, including: clairvoyance, psychometry and precognition, who can sometimes communicate with spirits, ghosts or entities.

Quantum mechanics

Fundamental branch of physics with wide applications in experimental physics and theoretical physics that replaces classical mechanics and classical electromagnetism at the atomic and subatomic levels.

Reality

The term reality, in its widest sense, includes everything that is, whether it is observable, comprehensible, or apparently self-contradictory by science, philosophy, or any other system of analysis. Reality in this sense may include both being and nothingness, whereas existence is often restricted to being (compare with nature).

Reincarnation

Reincarnation, literally "to be made flesh again", is a doctrine or mystical belief that some essential part of a living being survives death to be reborn in a new body. According to such beliefs, a new personality is developed during each life in the physical world, but some part of the being remains constantly present throughout these successive lives as well.

Religion

A religion is a set of beliefs and practices generally held by a community, involving adherence to codified beliefs and rituals and study of ancestral or cultural traditions, writings, history, and mythology, as well as personal faith and mystic experience.

Residual Haunting

Experiences from the living that are imprinted in a specific location and are replaying on a cyclical basis, like the playback of a movie, such as apparitions doing the same things or voices and sounds being heard at always the same time of the day. Many hauntings can be of this sort and not necessarily animated by conscious spirits.

Ritual

A ritual is actually the words of a "rite", which are said as a part of a ceremony which is a set of actions, performed mainly for their symbolic value, which is prescribed by a religion or by the traditions of a community.

Sacred (Holiness)

Holiness, or sanctity, is the state of being holy or sacred, that is, set apart for the worship or service of God or gods. It is most usually ascribed to people, but can be and often is ascribed to objects, times, or places. The word holy is related to the word whole.

Satan
Satan, from the Hebrew word for "adversary", is a term that originates from the Abrahamic faiths, being traditionally applied to an angel. Religious belief systems other than Judaism relate this term to a demon, a rebellious fallen angel, devil, minor god and idolatry, or as an allegory for evil

Séance
A séance is an attempt to communicate with the dead. The séance, or sitting, is led by a person known as a medium who will usually go into a trance that theoretically allows the dead to communicate through him or her. The word séance comes from the French word for 'seat', 'session', from Old French seoir, 'to sit.' In English, the word came to be used specifically for a meeting of people to receive spiritualistic messages.

Seminar
A seminar is, generally, a form of academic instruction, either at a university or offered by a commercial or professional organization. It has the function of bringing together small groups for recurring meetings, focusing each time on some particular subject, in which everyone present is requested to actively participate.

Sleep paralysis
Sleep paralysis is a condition characterized by temporary paralysis of the body shortly after waking up (known as hypnopompic paralysis) or, less often, shortly before falling asleep (known as hypnagogic paralysis).

Soul
The soul, according to many religious and philosophical traditions, is the self-aware essence unique to a particular living being. In these traditions the soul is thought to incorporate the inner essence of each living being, and to be the true basis for sapience.

Smudging
A smudge stick is a bundle of dried herbs, most commonly white sage. Often other herbs or plants are used or added and the leaves are usually bound with string in a small bundle and dried. Ojibway and Cree ceremonies often use smudges of sage, sweet grass, and/or juniper to cleanse with, and to give prayers to the Creator, or Gitchee Manitou.

Spirit Guides
Term used by mediums and spirituals to describe an entity that remains a disincarnate spirit in order to act as a spiritual counsellor or protector to a living incarnated human being.

Spiritism

Spiritism is a philosophical doctrine akin to Spiritualism, established in France in the mid 19th Century, which has become a sort of religious movement. Like Spiritualists believe in the survival of the souls after death and the importance of eventual communications received from them. Spiritism derives most of its principles from works by the French educator Hippolyte Léon Denizard Rivail written under the pseudonym Allan Kardec.

Spiritualism

Spiritualism is a religious movement, prominent from the 1840s to the 1920s, found primarily in English-speaking countries. The movement's distinguishing feature is the belief that the spirits of the dead can be contacted by mediums. These spirits are believed to lie on a higher spiritual plane than humans, and are therefore capable of providing guidance in both worldly and spiritual matters. Spiritualism is closely related to Spiritism, a religious movement that originated in France, and is today widespread in Brazil and other Latin countries.

Spirituality

Spirituality, in a narrow sense, concerns itself with matters of the spirit. The spiritual, involving (as it may) perceived eternal verities regarding humankind's ultimate nature, often contrasts with the temporal, with the material, or with the worldly.

Spirituality often focuses on personal experience. Many spiritual traditions share a common spiritual theme: the "path", "work", practice, or tradition of perceiving and internalizing one's "true" nature and relationship to the rest of existence (God, creation (the universe), or life), and of becoming free of the lesser egoic self (or ego) in favor of being more fully one's "true" "Self".

Spiritual healing
Use of spiritual means in treating disease. Spiritual healing can also refer to the self-empowerment or self-actualization process or steps within those processes that often occurs with individuals seeking enlightenment or meaning in their lives.

Supernatural
The supernatural refers to forces and phenomena which are not observed in nature, and therefore beyond verifiable measurement.

Thanatology
Thanatology is the academic, and often scientific, study of death among human beings. It investigates the circumstances surrounding a person's death, the grief experienced by the deceased's loved ones, and larger social attitudes towards death such as ritual and memorialization.

Telepathy
Communication of information from one mind to another by means other than the known perceptual senses.

Theology
Theology finds its scholars pursuing the understanding of and providing reasoned discourse of religion, spirituality and God or the gods.

Tibetan Book of the Dead (Bardo Thodol)
The Bardo Thodol is a funerary text that describes the experiences of the consciousness after death during the interval known as bardo between death and rebirth. The Bardo Thodol is recited by lamas over a dying or recently deceased person, or sometimes over an effigy of the deceased.

Trance
An altered state of consciousness is any state which is significantly different from a normative waking beta wave state. A synonymous phrase is "altered states of awareness".

Wicca
Wicca is a religion found in various countries throughout the world. It was first popularized in 1954 by a retired British civil servant named Gerald Gardner after the British Witchcraft Act was repealed. He claimed that the religion, of which he was an initiate, was a modern survival of an old

witchcraft religion, which had existed in secret for hundreds of years, originating in the pre-Christian Paganism of Europe.

Witchcraft

Witchcraft is the use of certain kinds of alleged supernatural or magical powers. A witch is a practitioner of witchcraft. While the term "witchcraft" can have positive or negative connotations depending on cultural context, most contemporary people who self-identify as witches see it as beneficent and morally positive. The term witch is typically feminine, masculine equivalents include wizard, sorcerer, warlock and magician.

The first thing which I can record concerning myself is, that I was born. These are wonderful words. This life, to which neither time nor eternity can bring diminution - this everlasting living soul, began. My mind loses itself in these depths.

Groucho Marx

"We're merely one tree with various types, shapes, and sizes of leaves that all wave differently in the breeze."

- Rashid Ogunlaru